NIPPER tHe ZIPPER
aNd HOWDY TATTOO

NIPPER the ZIPPER
and HOWDY TATTOO

WRITTEN by MARIAN KELNER
ILLUStRATED by NANCY B. BAKER

ISBN 978-0-9969719-8-0
Printed in the United States

Ginger Cat Design: Booksmyth Press
Shelburne Falls, MA
www.gingercatdesigns.biz

DEDICATED TO

all the creatures of the sea
and all who try to help them

Nipper the Zipper and Howdy Tattoo

go sailing one day in a boat made of glue.

They don't get very far. They're stuck where they are.

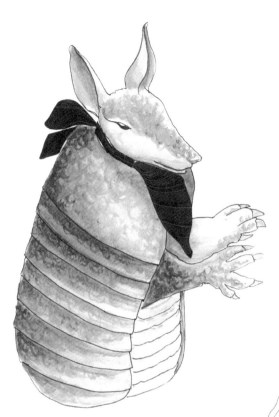

"What shall we do?"
asks Howdy Tattoo.

"Can't say," mumbles Zip.
"The glue's got my lip!"

A dolphin swimming gently nearby

sees this big mess and gives out a cry.

"I'll help you gladly, I always do,

if you'll never again make a ship out of glue.

"We promise, we promise, we give you our word,

as best as we can, if we can be heard."

The dolphin smiles and knows it's true,

if she takes them out of that gooey glue

they would see how smart those who swim can be

and devote their lives to protecting the sea.

And here's what happened from her good action

in Howdy and Zipper's amazing reaction.

They now walk the beaches combing the shore

picking up plastic wherever they are.

They bring most to a recycling center

but keep some so they can enter

projects for sculptures

made of pieces of plastic

in shapes of sea life that are truly fantastic.

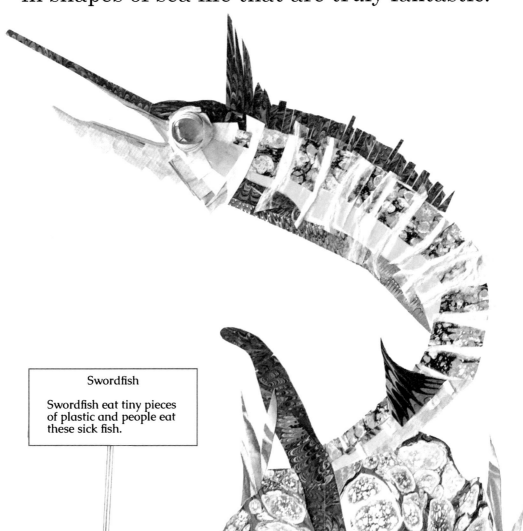

Swordfish

Swordfish eat tiny pieces of plastic and people eat these sick fish.

The sculptures show how much plastic there is
that washes ashore in the foam and the fizz.

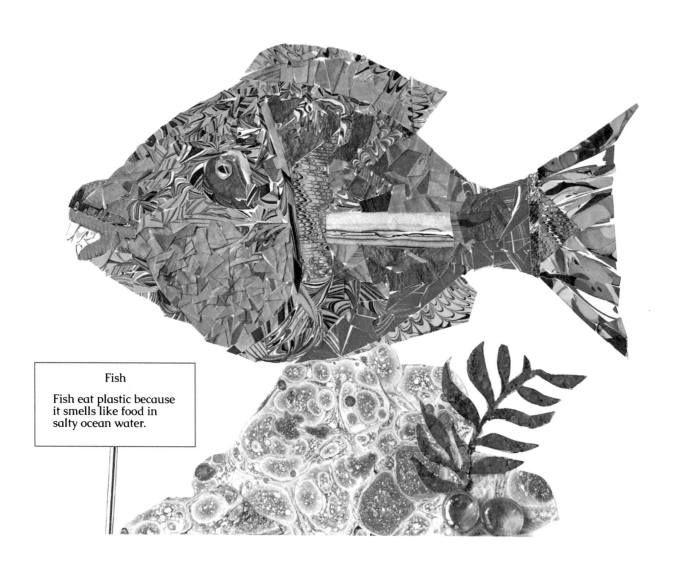

Fish

Fish eat plastic because
it smells like food in
salty ocean water.

They teach people how harmful this plastic can be when it ends up in rivers, oceans and seas.

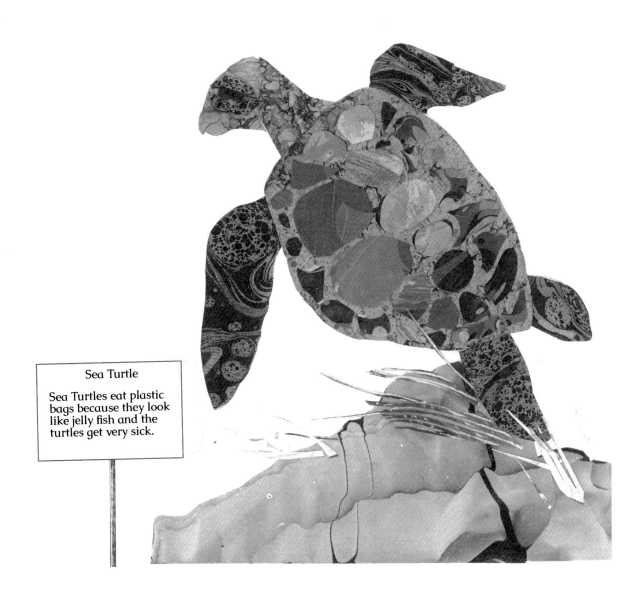

Sea Turtle

Sea Turtles eat plastic bags because they look like jelly fish and the turtles get very sick.

Now around the world more people are walking

picking up plastic while others are gawking

until they realize what needs to be done

and join in to help while still having fun.

Maybe one day there will be no more plastic

no free-floating garbage and the ocean at last is

clean and pure for all the plants and fishes.

Do you want to help to fulfill these wishes?

How You Can Help

Recycle everything – even plastic bags

Use your own reusable water bottle

Use paper straws, not plastic ones

Leave wildlife, like frogs and small fish,

in their homes

Choose products that do not use plastic wrapping

Wherever you go, take all your toys and garbage

with you when you leave

Turn the water off when brushing your teeth

Reuse what you have instead of buying something new

Learn about the oceans and those who live in them

Participate in local beach cleanups

Thank you from Nipper the Zipper and Howdy Tattoo

and all who live in the oceans, lakes, and rivers!

A special thank you

to

Washed Ashore

for their permission to base

our illustrations of sculptures

on their work.

Visit their website at

https://washedashore.org/

You will be amazed

and learn a lot!

MARIAN KELNER is the author of three books of collected writings and a songwriter with two CDs. As first and foremost a living being in this miraculous cosmos, she does her best to advocate for our beautiful Earth and the beings who are trying to share it with us humans. She lives in Western Massachusetts with her cat, Mouse. Her website can be found at www.mariankelner.net.

NANCY B. BAKER received her BFA from Washington University School of Fine Arts in 1965 and has been creating art in different media ever since. She has murals in many parts of the United States and in Brazil. She is a member of the Shelburne Arts Co-op where much of her work is exhibited. Her focus is the natural world and in particular birds and animals. Her website can be found at www.artscoop.com. She and her husband reside in Greenfield, MA.

97656068R00019

Made in the USA
Lexington, KY
01 September 2018